To Sandra
Dare to dream BIG!
God is truly able.

DREAMS, HOPES AND POSSIBILITIES

A breast cancer survivor's story of a dream come true

Peace, love and blessings,
Paula

Paula Smith Broadnax

Jackie S. Henderson, MDiv, DMin
YOUR FAMILY RESEARCH & PUBLISHING
Stone Mountain, GA

Paula Smith Broadnax

Dreams, Hopes and Possibilities
A breast cancer survivor's story of a dream come true

ISBN-13:978-1492109198

ISBN-10:1492109193

Cover Photo designed by Tommie Broadnax

Jackie S. Henderson, MDiv, DMin
YOUR FAMILY RESEARCH & PUBLISHING
Stone Mountain, GA

Printed in the United States of America

PREFACE

My desire was to seek God's guidance and wisdom as I moved to make my dream a reality. I know that wisdom is found in His Word (the Bible) and through prayer. The following scripture reminded me of what I should do and how I must proceed in order to be within the will of God.

His Word tells us in Hebrews 13:1-2 to *"Let brotherly love continue. Be not forgetful to entertain strangers; for thereby some have entertained angels unawares."*

During December 2007, one of my spiritual advisors, Rev. Dennis Mitchell of Greenforest Community Baptist Church in Decatur Georgia, preached a series of sermons that dared us to move forward with what God had planted in our minds to do. For me, that meant to write my story of how I had lived my dream!

Rev. Mitchell challenged us by saying, "Don't be afraid to DREAM or have a vision." He added there is HOPE in a dream, but our dream must be Christ-centered and driven by a passion to make a difference in the lives of others. He further encouraged us to dream of the POSSIBILITIES.

In the sermon series, we were admonished to "tell our God story." This is my desire for this book. I want to let others know that "All things are possible to those who love the Lord." Let me assure you...I truly love the Lord! I know for a fact that God hears and answers prayers.

My story is that of an answered prayer, fulfilled in part by so many who were praying for and with me. Rev. Mitchell reminded us that "Wise men and women continue to seek God."

I hope that what I have to share will encourage others to move forward with the dreams God has given them and not to be afraid. I want to encourage them to write the vision and make it plain because as God gives the vision, He also makes the provision.

Habakkuk 2:2-3 states, *"And the Lord answered me and said, write the vision: make it plain upon tables that he may run and readeth it. For the vision and yet for an appointed time, but at the end it shall speak, and not lie; though it tarry, wait for it; because it will surely come, it will not tarry."*

Seek God continually and move forward knowing that if you take one step, He'll take two! Seek opportunities to share with others along the way of how God is blessing you to be able to work toward the dream He has given. Remember, where there are DREAMS, there is HOPE; and where there is HOPE, there are POSSIBILITIES!!

DEDICATION

This book is dedicated to my Mother, Bessie Lee Smith; and my son, Darryl Lamar Daugherty, Sr. both of whom have gone to be with the Lord. They are guiding and cheering me all the way.

It is also dedicated to all breast cancer survivors. Dare to dream as you give hope to others while moving through your challenges, knowing that all things are possible with God.

Paula Smith Broadnax

Dreams, Hopes and Possibilities

CONTENTS

Chapter   Page

ACKNOWLEDGMENTS

I want to thank the following people who have helped me along the journey:

My helpmeet and wonderful husband, Tommie Broadnax, (the missing link) who believed in the fulfillment of my dream and who wholeheartedly supported it.

Bessie Lee Smith, my mother, for instilling strong spiritual values in me, blessing me and the vision, as well as encouraging me to go forward.

My sister in Christ, Kathryn "Kitty" Anderson for sharing the dream with me from the beginning and helping to get things moving.

Barbara Welch, my dear friend, for her love and support... always!

TooWah Ra'Atum of G.I.G. Photography, the best photographer I know!

Dr. Jackie Henderson of Your Family Research and Publishing for believing that now is the time for the story to be told and making it happen.

A host of friends and loved ones who saw the dream with me and believed that I could and would do it.

And last, but not least, my family, for supporting me and one another while I was away doing "my thing!"

A very special thank you to my brother, Warren Thomas Smith, Jr. and my beloved sister-in-law, Joy, for being the glue that kept things together. I love you both dearly!

FOREWORD

My wife Nolly, short for Noelia, and I received a telephone call one afternoon from a couple with a strange surname, Broadnax. They said that they were visiting St. Croix, U.S. Virgin Islands and had been referred to me by my cousin, Sondra Howard. It is ironic that Sondra had recently visited St. Croix and was now Paula Smith Broadnax's replacement at AT&T (from which Paula had just retired).

During one of their last conversations on the job, Paula mentioned her dreams of moving to St. Croix. Sondra told Paula to be sure to look up her island cousin, Richard Austin, when she came to St. Croix. She did and we invited them to our home for dinner. This is the origin of my first encounter with Paula and Tommie Broadnax and their **DREAMS, HOPES AND POSSIBILITIES**, which is the subject of this inspiring, must read book.

It is my understanding that Paula's dream of owning a Bed and Breakfast in the Caribbean was borne many years earlier. I had the privilege to officiate the blessing and grand opening ceremony of InnParadise Bed and Breakfast Inn. This was the dream that came true for Paula and Tommie.

I served as their pastor during their stay on St. Croix and have many fond and proud memories of events and people that I met at the Inn. There were poetry readings, musical recitals, birthday parties, dinners, and other community events.

Paula's southern smothered fried chicken, and grits & gravy were always a hit with the guests. And I always welcomed an invitation to partake! There were always many interesting guests and celebrities like actor Danny Glover to meet at the Inn.

Oops … I dropped one name and I do not want to mention others because I want you to hear from Paula in the pages of this book. This book is a wonderful example of love, faith and determination.

It highlights how one should never give up on accomplishing his dreams. In spite of many obstacles in her way—illness, death, financial barriers—Paula always displayed a faithful approach in her actions.

In a world filled with negatives, it is a delight to explore the pages of **DREAMS, HOPES AND POSSIBILITIES.** So enjoy, and may the Good Lord Bless You Richly!

Rev. Richard Austin, Esq., Pastor
Beulah AME Zion Church
St. Croix, Virgin Islands

Paula Smith Broadnax

CHAPTER 1

IN THE BEGINNING

Habakkuk 2:2-3

"And the Lord answered me and said, write the vision and make it plan upon tables that he may run and readeth it. For the vision and yet for an appointed time, but at the end it shall speak, and not lie; though it tarry, wait for it; because it will surely come, it will not tarry."

Kathryn and Paula

My sister Kathryn Yarbough Anderson (lovingly known as Kitty) and I were talking one day when she said "I have always desired to live on an island." I responded, "Really? And I would love to own a bed and breakfast inn!" Kitty's reply, "You know, we could own a bed and breakfast inn on an island." It all began by simply speaking those words!

A friend had reminded me one day, I had spoken about that desire back in the 1980's. I don't really remember doing so, but what I do remember is that from the time of my youth, our home had always been a haven for all people.

My mother cooked all the time and our community knew they were welcome to drop in at any time. Everyone knew where to go to get a piece of the best sweet potato pie during the holidays; or a glass of delicious, homemade grape wine when the vines in our backyard were ripe. When I became an adult, my home was the place for the annual Kentucky Derby parties, frequent gatherings to play Trivial Pursuit, and just the all around place to gather.

During this time, my girlfriends and I took frequent vacations to the Bahamas to attend annual conferences sponsored by The Black Career Women headquartered in Cincinnati, Ohio.

My girlfriends and I were lovingly known as "The Golden Girls" because of the unique complimentary personalities of the five of us (which included our flair, our love of fashion, and the genuine fun we always had when we were together).

Paula Broadnax, Margaret Harris, and Terri Broadnax

Paula Smith Broadnax

MORE PICTURES OF THE GOLDEN GIRLS

Margaret Harris, Paula Broadnax, Terri Broadnax

Arnhill Rumsey and Mary Porter

On every visit without fail, several Bahamians would mistake me for a cousin of theirs. They made me feel like family (which we are). I believe this is around the time that I realized I was attached to the Caribbean. I have always had a love for the people, food, music and the water.

Kitty tells how she remembers the idea of owning a bed and breakfast inn came about ...

I came to Atlanta in May, 1988 and visited with the Greenforest Baptist Church from that time until my official joining in September, 1988. It was at that time that I met Paula Daugherty at the New Members Group meeting/Sunday School class. Paula made me feel a part of my new home at Greenforest.

Paula (Daugherty) Broadnax

As the months went on, I decided to join the choir of which Paula was a part. We seemed to take to each other and I was appreciative of the fact that Paula tried to include me in social activities that she was a part of. Not only did we become good friends, but I believe we were also on the same spiritual communication line with one another. We went to Wednesday Night Bible Study and we also had our own Bible Study over the phone each week, taking turns reading a specific Book of the Bible that we chose together to study.

As time progressed in Atlanta, GA, I don't recall us having a discussion about our "Hopes and Dreams" but we seemed to be on the same wave-length anyway. My first recollection of us having a discussion was in September, 1994. But before that time, I had decided that I would like to treat myself to a very nice 50th Birthday celebration which was coming up on August 5, 1994.

Kitty, Paula & Sheri

In September of 1993, I decided to plan for my trip to St. Thomas, USVI for my 50th birthday treat. In sharing my thoughts with Paula, she said that I could not go to St. Thomas to celebrate by myself. In any case, I was told by Paula that she was not going to be left behind and was going to accompany me on my birthday trip.

Needless to say, Paula thought it was a good idea to invite other close friends to join us for the celebration. In total, there were seven of us flying to St. Thomas for my birthday. We left on August 3rd, a Wednesday, and returned on Sunday, August 7th, staying at the Wyndham Sugar Bay Resort.

On Sunday morning, the last day of our stay, I went to the restaurant for breakfast. There I met a young man. He was very personable and, since I was sitting by myself, invited me over to have breakfast with him and his cousin. We talked about my visit and I told him I was here with friends.

In any case, he invited me and the other six to join him at Coki Point which was just about a quarter of a mile away from the hotel. He was going to take a swim. I called everyone on the phone for one last dip in the ocean before taking our 4:00 PM flight back and we all piled into his car to take us to the beach.

In our conversation, we found out that he was a helicopter pilot with the Army Reserve and lived on St. Croix and invited us to visit soon. He indicated that St. Croix was a bedroom community compared to St. Thomas and was much prettier, quieter, had rolling hills, and was less populated than St. Thomas. As Paula and I engaged him in conversation about St. Croix, he asked us when we were leaving the island.

Since we were leaving later that day, he offered to pick us up and take us to the airport. During our ride, he would further tell us more about St. Croix. On the way to the airport, he made a stop at a relative's house. This is where we were introduced to his cousin, Jack, who was an excellent island carpenter. After this, we all hopped on the plane to return to Atlanta.

After we returned from vacation, we reminisced about our fun trip, the people we met, and then settled back into our routine. As usual, Paula and I had our discussions over the phone and, one of the discussions, as I recall it, was in September of 1994 when Paula said that one of her dreams was to own a bed and breakfast inn. I told her that since I loved the beach and warm weather so much, I wanted to have the experience of living on an island.

I then got the bright idea and said, "Why don't we have a bed and breakfast inn on an island? That way, we could both accomplish our desires." We laughed and said it sounded like a good idea. Surprisingly, after some thought, we both agreed to seriously investigate the possibilities and, before we knew it, we were "running with it".

From that discussion, Paula found a six-week course entitled "So You Want to be an Innkeeper" being held at Oglethorpe University. The course cost us about $60.00 each. We then began to seriously read all that we could put our hands on, purchasing various books on the subject.

One day, Paula mentioned to me that Rev. Myles Munroe was speaking at New Birth Missionary Baptist Church on "Your Purpose in Life" and, based on the subject matter of the 3-day speaking engagement, we should go to hear him, hoping that we would get some words of encouragement. After hearing Rev. Munroe speak, we were further encouraged and felt we were on the right track. Words that we derived from Rev. Munroe that we took as our banner and staff were:

"Plan with Purpose,

Prepare with Prayer,

And Proceed Positively in Persistent Pursuit of Your Goal."

One of the chapters from Dr. Munroe's book,[1] entitled "In Pursuit of Purpose" indicates some of the principles that we followed. These were:

"Purpose and Vision Principles

1.   Purpose creates a vision.

2. Vision produces goals.

3. Goals determine the necessary steps toward the desired end; goals dictate companions; goals determine decisions; goals predict choices; goals create priorities; goals provide a measure for progress.

4. A plan incorporates and unifies the designated steps toward the efficient fulfillment of purpose."

---

[1] Munroe, Myles. *In Pursuit of Purpose*. Pennsylvania: Destiny Image Publishers Inc., 1992.

Sometime in the late Fall of 1994, we decided that we would make contact with a realtor on the island of St Croix to investigate the island to see if St. Croix would be the right place. I found a few names online for realtors and decided to contact Mr. Roland Groder.

I spoke with Roland and told him of our desires to look around the island for a piece of property that could serve as a bed and breakfast inn. I also indicated that we would not be able to visit until the spring of next year, 1995. I continued to stay in contact with Roland, who was very diligent and stayed in contact with us from start to finish and beyond. Roland and Susan Groder turned out to be great friends.

Paula and I continued to work on the project and on April 25, 1995, we were booked to leave for St. Croix on a Wednesday and returning from St. Thomas on the following Sunday afternoon. Our plan was to have a full day with Roland on Thursday on St. Croix Island and then fly out to St. Thomas on Friday morning and stay until Sunday.

As we were preparing our trip, Paula invited her cousin, Mary Johnson, to travel with us and meet us on St. Croix. We all stayed at the Christiansted Hotel in the downtown area for two nights (Wednesday and Thursday), departing on Friday morning.

Roland met us at the hotel on Thursday morning and gave the three of us the grand tour of the island. We first went to "The Breakfast Club" Bed and Breakfast Inn and met with the owners, Toby and Barbara, who showed us around the place and what it had to offer.

We were impressed with the property, especially with the view of the ocean. Roland then took us to other places as we rounded the island.

We eventually worked our way over to Frederiksted and looked at some properties there. We had lunch in the Rain Forest area. We made a lunch stop at a place called the Domino Club where they had two large pigs who drank beer. It was quite amusing and we all had fun.

Beer-drinking pig

I think we were especially impressed with Roland, how he seemed to get along with the locals, how easy-going, patient, friendly, and honest he appeared to be (and we were right). We again stopped at other locations as we neared Christiansted again, and had a wonderful day on the island which was well spent. We thanked Roland for his hospitality and told him that we would definitely like to stay in contact with him.

13

We all packed up and left on a Friday morning flight to St. Thomas, USVI. To our surprise, we arrived on the island when Carnival was in full force. After checking in to the Mafolie Hotel, we were not comfortable with our situation as unaccompanied ladies and asked that the manager secure us another hotel. We were able to obtain housing at Bluebeard's Castle Hotel. Luckily for us, it turned out to be wonderful.

We had a large room with a very nice patio and we were able to get a roll-away cot for Mary to sleep on. Since we did not have any contacts for realtors on St. Thomas, we just toured the sights and watched the Carnival parade. While we were on the island, we also ran into local islanders who we had met the previous year for my birthday celebration.

CHAPTER 2

HOW I MET MY HUSBAND

My sister, Sharon, had called to say she was having a housewarming and birthday celebration and she wanted me to come. I am more of a planner and she does things more spontaneously.

So I was looking for a way to get out of going to the party because it was a cold November night and I was comfortable at home in front of the fireplace with a glass of wine. I can hear my mother saying now ..."Girl, you know that your sister is going to be mad at you if you don't go!" So I decided to go to please mama.

I dressed up to go make an appearance. Since it was a party, I dressed for such ….remember…. I am a "Golden Girl" (that says I was overdressed for some people…..large earring, chic pants suit with a wide, tight belt and a mink coat……it was cold outside!!)

I was late arriving, of course, and the party was in full swing with lots of people everywhere. Sharon was excited to see me and took me around the room introducing me to her guests. After we had made our way around the room, we came to a handsome gentleman. It turns out his name was Tommie and he attended Hillside Truth Center with Sharon and her husband, TaKuma.

Tommie was in the Men's Ministry with TaKuma who had invited him to the event. Tommie offered me his seat. I sat there for a moment and got up to go talk to some of the other guests. After I had "worked the room" (as Tommie has come to term my actions at a party), I returned to find him still standing along the wall.

He was quite interesting to me and I enjoyed our conversation. I thought "I would not mind getting to know him better;" however, it was late for me and I was ready to return home. I had forgotten to bring my business cards with me so, I went to Sharon's room and wrote my name and phone number on a piece of paper…..just in case he asked for it☺.

When I told him I was leaving he said "I would like to keep in touch with you. May I have your number?" I said, "Sure, I would like that." Now, our recollections differ here; but Tommie says I whipped out my information like "Quick Draw McGraw"! Do you remember who that was?? By the way…. I did not! I just gave him the paper ☺.

Tommie's recollection of how we met…

In August of 1995, I found myself in the middle of a protracted divorce and living with my daughters and one grand-daughter. After fourteen years of marriage, I decided that if I were to meet someone else it would strictly be for the occasional dinner date or movie; not that I was in a hurry to meet someone you understand.

As things would have it, it was not convenient to continue attending my old church and I was introduced to Hillside Chapel and Dr. Barbara King. After visiting for just two weeks, I joined the church and started their New Members' Class.

It seemed that Hillside was the answer to my prayers. I had been going through a lot of self evaluation and was seeking a new direction in my life. The philosophy at Hillside was different from my past church experiences and really fed my spirit.

In November, I was invited to join the Men's group at their weekly fellowship and holiday luncheon. I was introduced to a great bunch of men dedicated to God and the Church. Midway through the luncheon, we received word that our Pastor was not pleased at not being invited to our fellowship.

Her comment was that "Had she been a male she would not have been excluded!" She however did stop by and offered a word of prayer and two bits of prophesy. The first was that someone in the group would experience an increase in their business endeavors. The second was that someone in the group would meet a very special woman.

Near the end of the fellowship, a brother known as TaKuma aka "Kingman," mentioned that he was having a holiday and birthday celebration for his wife, Sharon, and that we were all welcome to come. Being new to the group and thinking that this would be a good occasion to meet other people, I said that I would see him later that evening.

After getting home and settled, the weather turned quite cold and I began to talk myself out of going. My daughters, on the other hand, were determined that I go out and stop spending so much time at home!

I got dressed and headed out. I arrived at the affair and was introduced to a very eclectic group of people; artist, musicians, writers and others. I was having a good time; but after eleven o'clock, I was starting to consider what time I would leave. Midnight and I'm still there and a very flamboyant woman makes an entrance.

It just happened to be the sister of the birthday celebrant. There were no seats left so I offered her mine and stood next to the wall. I noticed that this woman got up and engaged in conversation with a number of people and eventually wound up standing next to me.

After reintroducing herself as the sister of Sharon, we talked for a good while. Although I was initially put off by her entrance, after talking with her I found that she was very engaging and interesting. I knew I would be leaving soon and was about to ask for her phone number when she excused herself and went off with her sister.

I thought....darn, a missed opportunity! Shortly she returned and I asked for the number and she handed me a slip of paper. She explained that normally she carries business cards but, had left them home.

Our Conversations Continue ...

Tommie called a few days later and we talked for hours. He soon began to visit me at home where we talked about everything. He was so open and honest about his life. He told me about his childhood; family; and basically, his life and where he had come from. I must say that he did not hold anything back.

I remember thinking.....WOW! I can't believe he is sharing all this with me. Some of it was painful to him; but he felt he should tell me. Had we met earlier in my life and spiritual journey, I might not have been so willing to listen or would have possibly been judgmental.

What I know is that we all have a past and have come from somewhere. Who are we to judge one another because "all have sinned and fallen short of the glory of God." God forgives us and we must forgive ourselves and ask others for forgiveness.

Since, he was so open and honest...it lead me to do likewise. He made me feel safe.....like I could lay my heart in his hand and he would not squash it! You see....my life was quite content as it was. I was not looking for a boyfriend....I had my friend girls!

This was November 1995. After meeting Tommie, Kitty and I invited him to join us at some of the Holiday gatherings we were planning to attend. One was a play entitled "King of Glory" put on by a local church.

It was a very moving play and during the presentation there were times that the audience was standing, clapping and praising the Lord as we remember the birth of our Lord and Savior, Jesus Christ.

When I looked at Tommie, he was up singing, clapping and praising too! I looked at Kitty and winked! We had made a list of the traits we desired in our next mate. One of my desires was for the Lord to send me a spiritual Christian who would not be ashamed to worship and praise the Lord. Tommie had no problem doing so.

He attended several gatherings with us. Following each of them, it was like he did not want to go home (and neither did I)....so we would continue to talk and share with one another long after the events were over.....into the wee hours of the night.

I had scheduled a trip to Kentucky prior to the Holidays. On my trip I was quite excited about meeting Tommie and told my friends that I had met a nice man. I talked about him frequently while away.

I returned home on Christmas Eve....immediately call Kitty and invited her over. Tommie called to see if I had made it home safely. I invited him over too. The three of us were sitting by the fireplace talking and having a great time. Then he told me he had a present for me. When I opened it, I saw that it was something printed. I needed my glasses to see it.

Kitty had her glasses on, so I asked her to read it for me. She began reading it and then said.....I think Tommie should read this to you and I am going to leave so that he can! I thought....what is it?? It was a poem that he had written while I was away.

Well, Tommie had written me the sweetest poem and I would like to share it with you.

My spirit cried out to the God within
To fill the void

As my spirit awakened to the beauty of Gods' love
A yearning began to grow to share this wonderful gift

As I prayed my desire for companionship
My still small voice said wait, be patient

And then one day events combined to set the stage for us to meet

Without any difficulty our spirits sought each other out
Love found love, even before our human minds could
conceive it

You are more than I could have ever asked God for
For truely God knows my needs better than I

It is Gods' design that we walk in each others footsteps
Sometimes I lead and sometimes I follow

Life has taught me that the greatest gift is love
And I will share as much of my love as you are willing
and capable of accepting

And my heart is open to receive all the love
that you could possibly give

Thank you for being you
Thank God for His devine purpose

Tommie Broadnax
8-23-95

Original Poem Written by Tommie Broadnax for Paula

I was smitten.....he writes poetry! He told me he was a carpenter by trade. Well it turns out he did all types of home repairs. Our hot water heater went out. I told my mother, I was not sure what to do. I mentioned it to Tommie and he replaced it. My mother was impressed. She used to say...."That Tommie uses his head for more than just a head rest"!

Tommie began to come over every evening after work. We would talk for hours and I would have to send him home so I could get ready for the next day. After a few months it was evident to us that we wanted to be together.

I had been divorced for 18 years and was perfectly content with my life as it was. However, I knew that at some point I wanted to share my life with the right person and I believed that Tommie was that person. We decided that we were going to marry. When I told my mother, she was so happy and gave us her blessing. She loved Tommie, too! I believe that God had spoken to her telling her to get me to that party ☺.

We spent an enormous amount of time talking and sharing with one another. He was very open and honest with me about his life from childhood until now. He was so honest with me it was almost scary!

Paula Smith Broadnax

"I was content with my relationships at that time. Kitty and "The Golden Girls" (who are my Louisvillian friends from many years ago) were my traveling companions, confidants, and encouragers. However, I knew at some point I would be open to sharing my life with the godly man whom God placed in my life.

We were married May 4, 1996. Yes, about five months after meeting! It's been 17 years now and it is truly a blessed marriage. I cannot imagine my life without him!

Wedding Day (Tommie & Paula Broadnax)

During our wedding vows he recited a revised version of the original poem he had written for me. The audience could not hear him clearly and many asked for a copy of it which we later provided to all the guests. It follows:

(This is the addition to the Original Poem)

And as we set upon this course together
I pledge my love and life to you
To be all that God has made me to be
That helpmeet that God has promised you
To be by your side forever!
                    Tommie Broadnax
                    05-04-1996

CHAPTER 3

KITTY'S DETOUR

Kathryn (Yarbough) Anderson

Kitty speaking ...

In the latter part of 1995, I was beginning to feel my calling to fulfill my dream of being involved in Missions full-time.

In March of 1996, I went to a Missions Workshop, filled out my application and submitted it to the International Mission Board of the Southern Baptist Convention. I was subsequently invited to a Missions weekend conference in Richmond, VA in July. I accepted my assignment to go to Seoul, South Korea in August, 1996.

In December 1996, we made another trip to St. Thomas with Tommie to view property. We wanted Tommie to assess the situation and give his opinion and the workability of the idea regarding the Breakfast Club bed and breakfast inn and any other property we would encounter during the trip.

At that time we arranged to meet with Jack, the carpenter who was living on Jost Van Dyke in the British Virgin Islands. Jack was very knowledgeable about island construction. We stopped at Magen's Bay and sat on a picnic bench to discuss our vision. While there, an artist by the name of John Mangel, was sketching us and later painted a picture of the scene which Paula purchased.

This was a very important meeting because we were all fired up! Evidently, the artist could see and feel the positive energy exhuming from us because he was lead to capture the scene. Before leaving I asked him what he planned to do with the painting when he completed it. I gave him a business card and asked him to contact me if he planned to sell it. It was a year or so before I heard from him.....following is the photo of his completed work ... a captured moment in our history! Paula later purchased this piece which she still has hanging in her home.

Friends at Magens, Oil painting by John Mangel, Magens Bay St. Thomas, VI, December 1996

From St. Thomas, we headed to St. Croix for a look-see. I had gotten in contact with a Cruzan businessman we knew and asked if he would be so kind as to come in his plane from St. Croix to St. Thomas to pick us up and fly us back to St. Croix for two nights. He was gracious enough to pick us up. We were careful to bring only one small travel bag per person, since the plane was small and we did not want to be overloaded.

It was my first time in a small 4-seater but we all enjoyed the half-hour ride. We toured the island again with Tommie. This trip was primarily to show him why we had decided that St. Croix was the place. After talking to people and doing our research, we decided it would be better to stay within U.S. jurisdiction because the real estate and business laws were familiar to us.

We stayed at The Breakfast Club to see how it would feel to be a guest and to fantasize about owning it. The Banana Pancakes were delicious and we ate them every morning.

On that Sunday, we flew back to St. Thomas. We offered to pay for the gas and landing fees, but he declined. We then headed back to Atlanta from there.

We purchased a book entitled, "The Settlers' Guide" while on the island. This manual provided the information we needed to know about relocating to an island; i.e., securing a driver's license, the weather/climate; suggestions on furnishings, and much more.

In January 1997, I went to Mission School for three weeks and then was off to Seoul, South Korea on January 30, 1997 for the next two years. I worked at the International Mission Board.

Paula Smith Broadnax

Paula came to visit me in Korea in late April 1998 and stayed for two weeks, departing around May 8th.

Everything was still on track at that point until in or around October, I made a conscious decision not to partner with Paula and Tommie on the business venture. I chose to come home to Atlanta in December to re-evaluate my life and vision for my future – be it in Missions or otherwise.

After much prayer about my future, I chose to move to St. Croix in February to join Tommie and Paula. In July of 1999, I made the decision to return to Atlanta in early October 1999 to resume life there.

Little did I know at the time that my original prayer and request of God to live on an island had been answered two years ago, and it had nothing to do with the island of St. Croix.

When I returned to Atlanta, I was once again totally dependent on God's mercy, which is where He always wants us to be so that He can use us to the fullest for His glory. In submission to Him, He brought Edward Anderson into my life to give me that which was missing – a lifelong companion. We were married on June 23, 2001. Edward is the love of my life, makes me feel complete, and God continues to get the glory.

To my amazement on December 11, 2007, I realized that God had already answered my request by sending me to the peninsula of South Korea . A peninsula is a piece of land which is surrounded by water on three sides. Added to that, I lived and worked on the Island of Yoido, which is just across the river from the mainland of Seoul City. God had already spoken and gave me the desires of my heart in August, 1996 when I accepted the assignment to go to South Korea (not quite as I had envisioned it, but it was an answer to my wanting to live on an island and be involved in Missions). WOW! Isn't God AWESOME!

Edward and Kathryn Anderson

CHAPTER 4

THE DIAGNOSIS

The pivotal point in my life (which propelled me forward with my dream) was the diagnosis of breast cancer in May 1997. I had been prone to developing cysts in my body causing me to have a hysterectomy early in my 30's. I went into the hospital after a cyst had been aspirated. Following that procedure I developed a pain in that very area.

Upon contacting my doctor, she recommended that it be removed. I was admitted to the hospital for the removal of the cyst. When the cyst was sent to pathology...we got the news. This time it was different. Dr. Rogsbert Phillips informed us that it was cancerous! I went numb and zoned out. I think I was in shock! Tommie was right by my side, holding my hand and listening for me because I could no longer hear anything.

I was finally able to collect myself. Then I said....what do we do! She recommended doing a lumpectomy which is breast-conserving operation in which the surgeon removes the tumor together with some normal breast tissue surrounding it. Chemo and radiation were the courses of action my physician recommended.

I have always been quite healthy. My family called me "pleasingly plump" because of my body structure. I do believe that being healthy helped me to move through this experience in a way where I did not appear to be sick. I was so blessed. I do not remember losing my appetite. And I did not lose any weight. I cut my hair and began wearing a low afro in anticipation of loosing my hair. I must tell you that none of my hair came out. I continued to wear the afro for many years because it was low maintenance and many said becoming to me because of my facial features.

I chose to delay starting the treatments because in June 1997 one of the Golden Girls (Terri) was getting married. She was marrying Tommie's brother, whom she had met at our wedding. Of course, I wanted to be a part of her special day.

Paula Smith Broadnax

Before I started treatments, I felt it would be good for me to get away to meditate and pray. Being the eldest daughter of six children, I had always felt responsible for my family and the world at large. At this point I felt depleted physically, mentally and spiritually. I had always put myself last and I knew that if I was going to be healed....I must begin to think of myself first!

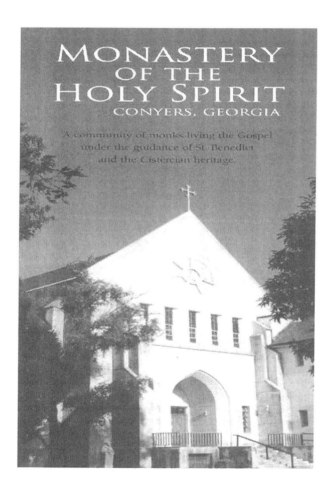

I found a monastery nearby. The Monastery of the Holy Spirit is located in Conyers, Georgia, 35 miles east of Atlanta. It was founded in 1944 by Cistercian-Trappist monks of the Abbey of Gethsemani located near Louisville, Kentucky. The members of this Order are cloistered, which means they do not leave the monastery precincts except when necessary and take part in no active ministry outside the Abbey.

This Order is a monastic institute wholly ordered to contemplation. The monks dedicate themselves to the worship of God in a hidden life within the monastery. They lead a monastic way of life in solitude and silence, in assiduous prayer and joyful penitence. Five times each day, beginning at 4:00 a.m., the monks assembly for community choral prayer.

Another one of the Golden Girls (Margaret) insisted on joining me because she did not want me to be alone. I am so glad that she came with me. It was one of the most spiritual encounters I have every had....the quietness, the early morning prayers, monks chanting, the lake and ducks.

Late one night, we became hungry and snuck down to the kitchen to get a peanut butter and jelly sandwich (on delicious homemade bread made by the monks). This was a "light" moment at a serious time in my life. I felt like a mischievous child ☺.

When we left, I was ready to go fight the cancer and I knew I would win!

Chemo began...it was not easy!   Eight weeks of treatment...weekly checkups to monitor my blood count and then the unthinkable happened.....My port got infected after the first treatment! I was devastated because it meant that it must be surgically removed and left open so that the infection could clear.

Now, I must admit that I am a wimp and queasy when it comes to blood, needles, etc. Walking around with an open whole in my chest was ghastly. Thank God for a strong husband. I believe he was practicing being a doctor on me because he handled every challenge with valor and even seemed to enjoy doing so.

I cannot imagine going through this experience without him in my life. God sends you who and what you need just when needed. After about a month of healing, I re-entered the hospital to have the port re-inserted. Then the radiation began....The body mold was made to ensure that I remained still during the treatments so that the proper area was treated each time. This was daily for two weeks. That was an experience in itself. My breast actually burned and the top layer of skin peeled off!

The only way I was able to bear this experience is because I was surrounded by so much love. Someone was always available to do whatever was needed. I never went to an appointment or treatment alone. My husband, sons, family and friends were always with me. My youngest son, Kyle, was very concerned about my well-being. I cannot thank him enough because he made himself available to go to most of my appointments with me. He loves me so much and I love him more.

My pastor from my church in Louisville, Kentucky even came to see about me. My co-workers came to visit and see what I might need. My inner circle was and is very tight. I was surrounded by so much love and support that I needed only to focus on me and my healing.

After I finished chemo and radiation, I claimed my healing and felt compelled to move forward with the vision. I was about to turn 50 and near the completion of a 30 year career with AT&T. But there was one thing that needed to be addressed. I felt that I needed my mother's permission. I did not feel like I could leave her.

My mother had lived with me for most of my adult life. Tommie and I talked with her and she gave us her blessing. She told me that I had taken care of everyone else all of my life and now it was time for me to do what I wanted. She was so full of wisdom and has instilled a strength in me that keeps me going today. Some of her wisdom is featured in a book written by Dennis Kimbro.[2]

---

[2] Kimbro, Dennis. *What Keeps Me Standing: Letters from Black Grandmothers on Peace, Hope and Inspiration*. Harlem Moon: New York, 2005, pp. 221-224.

CHAPTER 5

50TH BIRTHDAY......A MILESTONE

For my 50th birthday, my Mama decided to give me a surprise birthday celebration. I had always been the one to give the parties and she wanted to do something special for me. That made me feel special indeed. It was not a surprise because my sister-in-law, Mary, told me about it! Mama got so mad at her. Mary was going through some challenges and was not in her right mind evidently because if she was, she would have known not to do that to Miss Bessie! Mama eventually forgave her.

The party was awesome in so many ways....just to be alive was a blessing. Everyday is a birthday! My mother and close friends helped me celebrate a blessed day indeed.

Moving Forward ...

Tommie was excited about my dreams. He told me that he would follow me wherever I went. What more could a girl ask for! At this time, my mother lived with us. Bessie Lee Smith was a very special lady. I could not imagine leaving her, so I suggested to Tommie that we look stateside to see if we could find a suitable location.

Since I had gotten hooked on being near the water, for my 50th birthday, Tommie and I went to Jekkyl Island in September 1997. We stayed at a lovely bed and breakfast inn called the Rose Garden as we looked at properties. It was a wonderful time at a gorgeous antebellum home with great food and people.

However, when we went to the beach, the water was gray and the people were not warm like I had found people in the Caribbean to be. So I told Tommie, I did not think this would work for us.

After much prayer (and I had plenty of time to commune with God during this healing time), I believe that it was time to retire and move forward with the vision of establishing the inn. Several things had become very apparent to me: I was not Mother Teresa and responsible for the world. I should consider putting myself first instead of last. Finally, time was not promised to me. After much discussion with my husband, we agreed that it was time to move forward.

In December of 1997, Tommie and I made another trip to St. Croix. Prior to taking the trip I had already made arrangements for retirement. The person who replaced me was named Sondra. As I told her about my retirement plans, she got excited because she had a cousin residing on St. Croix.

I submitted my paperwork for retirement. I was only few months short of making my 30 years with AT&T. My retirement was approved; but I would have to take a penalty because I was a few months short of reaching 30 years. This was upsetting to me (as well as my peers) because we were aware of situations where exceptions had been made. I packed my desk and went home to continue moving forward. We were planning to trip to St. Croix and I was excited to be going back.

A few days later, I received a call from Headquarters informing me that my retirement had been approved at 30 years! Divine intervention, I believe! I was asked to return to work to train my replacement who turned out to be, Sondra. She had a cousin residing on St. Croix and suggested that we contact him when we arrived.

After returning from our trip, I returned to work to plan my retirement party. Since my replacement was already in place, I was able to ease my way through the following days. Now that is what I call God's favor.

Sondra provided contact information for Richard and Noelia (lovingly known as Nolly) Austin. They invited us to dinner. Nolly later told us that with a name like Broadnax, she was surprised that we were Black.

Richard is from Ohio and Nolly is originally from Puerto Rico. They have lived on St. Croix for a long time. As the Director of Legal Services for the entire U.S. Virgin Islands, Richard (and Nolly) are well known throughout the Virgin Islands and have many connections.

They adopted us and basically every event they were invited to, they included us (including the Governor's Ball, Senior's Community events, beach parties, jazz events, church and much more. This allowed us to get connected to the island people and it was great!

Richard was later ordained as an AME Zion minister and we included him in all of our activities warranting a minister. He was always delighted for the opportunity to do spiritual things for us and put his heart into it (including giving us printed copies of programs and prayers that he did for the occasions). Needless to say, we have become like brothers and sisters.

Equipping Ourselves ...

In February 1997, we attended the "Inn Deep Workshop" held in Cape May, NJ. Cape May is the bed and breakfast inn capital here in the states with a boardwalk to the gracious hospitality of Victorian Inns. Cape May County is a peninsula, located at the southernmost tip of New Jersey between the Atlantic Ocean and the Delaware Bay.

Seminar Attendees

We stayed at the Summers' Cottage Inn. The innkeepers were wonderful. I even got up one morning to help prepare breakfast for the guest and we purchased her cookbook. We also met other aspiring African American innkeepers.

I did research on the internet and found that there was a Professional Association of International Innkeepers (PAII). I also found that there was an African American owned inn in St. Louis, MO. We decided to visit a bed and breakfast inn owned by a lovely lady named Pam around Easter of 1998. She embraced us like family. In giving us a personal tour of her city, she would introduce us saying "These are the Broadaxes. They are going to open an inn in the Caribbean!" To hear her say that was music to our ears. Words are powerful and they do not return void!!

It is great when you can paint a picture and others see it with you. This is what helps you to move forward. You have more eyes and ears to bring you information and people resources. We shared a lot with Pam during this visit. Before we left she told me that she felt that Tommie was ready to go forward; but that I was hesitant....she was right! I did not want to leave my mother!

Towards the end of my career with AT&T, I worked as a Manager in the Career Resource Center. We offered courses to employees who were transitioning out of the company.

During this time, I had the opportunity to attend a course facilitated by Dr. Caela Farren entitled "Taking Charge of Your Career." We were challenged to envision where we saw ourselves 5, 10, 15 years from that point.

I painted a vivid picture for myself and was asked to share it with my classmates. I could see myself living in the Caribbean, opening my home to the world, and greeting my guests dressed in tropical attire, steel drums are playing in the background, and offering them a tropical beverage upon arrival. It was so real to me that I was able to convey this to my classmates and they were able to see me there too.

At the end of the course, many students came to me with their contact information asking me to please let them know of the inn opening!!! Now that is a vote of confidence!! I had no choice; but to go do it. BUILD IT …. AND THEY WILL COME!!

CHAPTER 6

RETIREMENT

I officially retired from AT&T in May 1998. As a retirement present, I went to visit Kitty in Korea. Tommie and I were moving forward and we needed to know if she desired to remain a part of the future plans. This was also a time for me to personally show the Missionary group an answered prayer. Kitty and the Missionaries had been praying for me as I went through the cancer battle. I could not wait to show and tell them what God had done in my life.

Visiting with Missionaries: Kathryn Anderson, Paula Broadnax, and Sheila Flowers

It was an awesome visit for me. One of the most memorable events was visiting Yoido Full Gospel Church, the largest church in the world. At that time, there were over 830,000 members, led by Reverend David Cho.

Founded in 1958, with five Christians attending the first service; the church sends out over 600 missionaries to preach

the gospel all over the world. It also makes great efforts to evangelize to Koreans with a goal of establishing over 500 new churches. Services were rendered in numerous languages. It was awesome to worship with Christians in another part of the world.

With the events that had recently occurred (getting married and being diagnosed with breast cancer), it felt like this would be a good time for me to move forward with my dream.

After thirty wonderful years with AT&T, I put in my paperwork to retire. I had begun working in Louisville, KY in 1965 as a stenographer with South Central Bell's Marketing Department. I was promoted to create and manage the Word Processing Center in 1985. Later I was promoted to Administrative Assistant to the Branch Manager of American Bell (short-lived) or AT&T.

Several consolidations occurred and I had an opportunity to move to Atlanta. I held numerous management positions in Finance (Internal Auditor); Human Resources (Relocation Counselor and Career Resource Manager).

AT&T had adequately equipped me with skills that I could use in creating my dream. I was excited about the opportunity to create my own business and do things "my way."

Paula Smith Broadnax

Pictures from AT&T Days

AT&T Marketing Department Word Processors

Auditing Standards and Principles Training, February 1992

CHAPTER 7

THE MOVE

Tommie and I sold our home and its contents because everything was changing for us and we did not want to hold onto material things. Our plans were to stay for ten years. We had already begun to change our mind set by simplifying our lives. We realize that the more we had, the more in time and money it took to maintain it.

Mama moved into an assisted living facility. The family vowed to be responsible for one another in my absence (particularly, mama and my sister, Gloria).

Tommie goes to St. Croix ...

After seeing Paula off to Korea, I boarded a flight to St. Croix. I arrived at the airport and called Roland, our realtor. He was surprised to hear from me because he had the wrong arrival date and was not expecting me. We had made arrangements with him to secure a condo.

Roland advised that he would have to collect the keys to the condo and agreed to meet me at McDonald's. We met and I was able to get settled in. It was a nice place near the beach and a small hotel call the Hibiscus.

For the first few days, I cleaned the condo, and took frequent walks on the beach and around the neighborhood. The friends we met earlier, Richard and Nolly, became my guides and helped me become acquainted with the island. In the three weeks I had before Paula's arrival I got phone and cable service established, retrieved our vehicles and personnel goods from the shipper, registered the vehicles and set up the condo.

When Paula arrived, we got down to the serious business of looking for the proper place to start the inn. Roland began to line up properties for us to see. After looking at a few, we realized that we needed to determine what would qualify as our future bed and breakfast inn.

Family is very important to us. During the next several months, several family members came to visit. Who wouldn't want to come visit family who lived on an island. Those who came were Bernita (Tommie's sister), Robert and Terri (Tommie's brother and his wife (a Golden Girl), Bill (my nephew), and Gloria (my sister).

Gloria

We wanted to remove as many obstacles as possible. We were advised that property would have to be zoned R3 or commercial. We needed to be in a community without an active homeowners association. Also, it had to feel right. After looking at a number of properties, it appeared that we were not going to find the property we were seeking.

Paula and I decided to make an offer on The Breakfast Club. With this being an established inn, we would take over an existing operation and not have to do everything from scratch.

But what we also recognized is that this inn did not represent us and our vision. We would have to do some major remodeling to make this truly our inn.

We hired a financial advisor to help prepare our presentation to the bank so that we would cover all of the bases. As time went on, the bank decided that they could not fund the project because the owner of the Breakfast Club could not document that his business was profitable enough to justify his asking price. We came to believe that he was doing quite a bit of cash business. We were willing to continue with this property if the owner would hold a small second mortgage with us. But he declined!

So, after nearly three months of looking, finding and being rejected, we found ourselves looking at properties once again. Paula and I continued to look for another three months. By this time, she was very frustrated. She was tired of the condo and wanted more space to stretch out.

Paula felt that we should find a small house, settle in, and continue looking. Not a good idea, but I decided to humor her. Roland lined up a few smaller houses to look at. I had been looking in property publications and noticed a property that seemed interesting. I asked Roland to include it in our trip for that day.

We looked at two or three small houses and Paula was not pleased at what was available for what we were willing to spend. Finally, we headed out to view the property of interest. We started up a hill, made a sharp right turn, continued uphill and over a rise and to our right sat a house with a covered carport.

Paula's first comment was that it looked like a "lodge." We walked up to a heavily carved wooden door and upon opening the door, we were greeted with a sight that took our breath away. We entered a large main room with sliding glass doors (ceiling to floor and wall to wall) that led to a large balcony. Through the glass doors was a view to die for! We looked down on the Caribbean Sea, Christiansted Harbor, and the Town Center. An artist could not have imagined a more beautiful and majestic view!

The realization to me was that now we were in paradise! I knew immediately that we had found the place to create our inn. It just happened that an agent in Roland's office held the listing. He called her to let her know that we were interested in the property.

The agent said that she had spoken to the owners just that morning. The house had been on the market for two years and they had decided to reduce the asking price by $10,000.00! We signed a contract that afternoon and felt that we were finally on our way.

Let me tell you more about this property. It had a large great room (which include a living room, dining room, kitchen and bar). There were three bedrooms and two baths, an office and a reading room on the main level. The lower level had a one-room suite on each end of the building, a laundry room, storage room and three cisterns. On the island, you collect rain water for your plumbing needs. The cisterns are built in the ground and ours were underneath the three bedrooms.

Each cistern could hold 3,300 gallons of water. There was a 16x30 pool and plenty of terraced green space. And there was no active homeowners association.

That's the good news! But it did not meet our zoning requirements. However, it felt right to us and we were moving forward. As we proceeded with the acquisition process, more problems were to develop. The survey revealed that we had some boundary disputes to clear up.

The house was being sold by the children of the owner who had passed on. The wife had divorced her husband and the property was "quit deeded" to the wife and there was an error in the deed. The bank had initially approved our loan, but decided to back out until the errors were corrected.

Operating strictly on faith and not wanting to lose the deal, we proposed to the owners that we would sign an agreement to purchase the property with the estate being the mortgage holder. The owners were to correct the errors in six months and we would then refinance the property.

Our friends thought we had lost our minds! Why would you continue with all the issues to be resolved?? We believed in our hearts that this is where God wanted us to create the vision. In late December 1998, we became the owners of the property now known as InnParadise. Hallelujah!

We moved in immediately and started the renovations. Paula returned stateside for some follow up medical appointments and I started to do what I do best -- demolition and reconstruction.

I ripped up carpet, tore out the old bar, got rid of the paneling on the walls, and started painting. Two weeks later, Paula returned to a freshly painted house with a "custom-made" bar. I had also built a dining room table and buffet.

Since we were starting this inn from scratch, we had to put in as much sweat equity as possible. I enjoyed working with wood and my previous business was remodeling homes. I was in my element!

Our plan was to complete the upstairs by June 1999 and be prepared to receive our first guest. As I was doing the remodeling based on Paula's decorating ideas, she began the process of getting the business end together.

In the six months that we had been on the Island, we had met a lot of people and we always talked about our plans. And in doing so, they were willing to do all they could to help us. An island is like any small town -- everybody knows everybody else!

The first thing we needed to do was to apply for a zoning change. We asked for advice from one of our friends and were told whom we should see. Upon arrival at the zoning office, they were expecting us. Our friend had already paved the way for us to begin the process. We applied for the zoning change and were advised that it could take as long as six months to get approval. However, we were allowed to secure our business license with temporary approval!

We had to get permission to use the name "InnParadise" and were initially rejected because someone on St. Thomas had filed to use the name "Paradise Inn." We could not use a like or similar name. There had never been a business license issued in the name of "Paradise Inn." We located the individual and confirmed they were not using the name, so we were allowed to start our business as InnParadise.

With our faith factor operating in high gear, we were well on our way to becoming innkeepers. We now own a piece of property that had some issues with the title. The survey shows that we have encroachment problems. The property is not zoned properly. But we had faith.

We are starting from scratch converting a single-family home into a bed and breakfast inn. From all of the research we had done, you would think that we had learned nothing and were fool heartedly proceeding. But, this is where our faith in Our Lord has led us and in our hearts we knew that this was the place.

We continued the renovations, started our website, and started purchasing furniture, supplies, appliances and the like to prepare to open our business in June. If everything proceeded as planned, all of the issues raised would be resolved, we would be re-financed, and the zoning would be approved. We would then be open for business.

April arrived and things are proceeding well. The two bedrooms on the main floor were complete. The common area was ready (except for about one hundred large pieces of tile that were stacked outside the door). We were preparing to do a large direct mail piece to all of the people who had expressed an interest in coming to our inn once we opened.

CHAPTER 8

OPEN FOR BUSINESS

<u>Hebrews 13:1-2</u>

"Let brotherly love continue. Be not forgetful to entertain strangers; for thereby some have entertained angels unawares."

Business Blessing …

I believe that all good and perfect gifts are from God. Everything that we have been entrusted with for this brief period of time belongs to Him. As we honor Him, we should give it back to him.

So, it was only fitting that we have a business blessing immediately upon moving into "InnParadise!"

We asked our friend, Rev. Richard Austin, if he would do the honors of blessing our business. He was very willing. We invited a few friends that we had met to join us.

Roland, our realtor, and Susan Groder

PRAYER OF DEDICATION AND BLESSING
FOR THE
INN PARADISE BED AND BREAKFAST
DECEMBER 27, 1998
ST. CROIX, VIRGIN ISLANDS

DEAR FATHER IN HEAVEN, WE COME NOW FIRST
GIVING YOU THE GLORY, HONOR, AND PRAISE, FOR
WHICH YOU ARE WORTHY. WE PRAY THIS PRAYER OF
DEDICATION AND BLESSING FOR THE SUCCESS OF THE
NEW BUSINESS ENTERPRISE TO BE OPERATED AT THIS
SITE BY YOUR SERVANTS, PAULA AND TOMMIE
BROADNAX, BY THE APPROPRIATE TRADE NAME, "INN
PARADISE , BED AND BREAKFAST. LORD, YOU HAVE
PREPARED BOTH OF THEM FOR THIS TASK BY
INSTILLING WITHIN THEM A GENUINE HEART OF LOVE
TOWARD OTHERS, AND A SINCERE SENSE, AND
UNDERSTANDING OF THE MEANING OF HOSPITALITY.

WE DEDICATE THIS BUSINESS TO THE GLORY OF GOD
AND TO HIS HONOR AS THE HEAD OF OUR LIVES. WE
FURTHER DEDICATE THIS BUSINESS TO THE HOPES AND
DREAMS OF PAULA AND TOMMIE FOR FUTURE PEACE,
PROSPERITY, HEALTH AND HAPPINESS IN THE
CONDUCT OF THIS NEW ENTERPRISE.

WE PRAY THAT AS THEY GO FORTH, THY PRESENCE
WILL GO WITH THEM. STRENGTHEN THEM IN THEIR
WEAKNESS, GUIDE THEM IN THEIR IGNORANCE, AND
INSPIRE THEM TO WILL AND DO ACCORDING TO THY

DIVINE GOOD PLEASURE. LORD, PLEASE MAKE THIS BUSINESS A PLACE OF PEACE, REST, ENTERTAINMENT, RECREATION AND SPIRITUAL ENLIGHTENMENT FOR ALL OF THE GUEST WHO WILL COME. WE PRAY THAT THE BUSINESS WILL HAVE SPIRITUAL AND FINANCIAL SUCCESS THAT WILL EXCEED PAULA AND TOMMIE'S GREATEST EXPECTATIONS. WE ASK THAT YOU BIND SATAN, AND ALL OF HIS EMISSARY, WHO WOULD STAND IN THE WAY OF THE SUCCESS OF THIS BUSINESS. MAY ILL-FORTUNE NEVER PREY UPON THIS ENTERPRISE.

NOW, GOD, MAY YOUR SPIRIT REST ON ALL OF YOUR PEOPLE, CAUSING US TO LEAD PEACEABLE, AND LOVING LIVES. BIND US TOGETHER BY THE BOND OF CHRISTIAN LOVE. HASTEN THE TRIUMPH OF THY KINGDOM HERE ON EARTH. THESE BLESSINGS WE ASK, WITH THE FORGIVENESS OF OUR SINS, IN THE PRECIOUS NAME OF OUR LORD AND SAVIOR, JESUS CHRIST, AMEN.

DELIVERED BY THE REVEREND RICHARD AUSTIN, ESQ.

We knew we were off to a great start following this ceremony!

We had met a lovely lady at church who has become known as our "island mother". Her name is Flossie and she was from Chicago and married to a local Cruzan (Mr. Hugo). She adopted us since we were from the states, and me from Illinois in particular. She was so proud of us and what we were planning to do on the island. She told all of her stateside friends and family that we were opening a "hotel."

Paula and Flossie

We had to explain to her what the concept actually was. One of her friends had been diagnosed with cancer and the wife was looking for a vacation for him. Flossie suggested they stay with us. We were not completely ready to receive guests.

Rooms were near ready; direct mailings were being done...and more.

So, our first guests arrived two months earlier than we had planned. They arrived at InnParadise in April 1999. No more practicing on our friends and people who we would pick up on the beach, but these were real paying guests. They were a delightful couple, Marvin and Ruth Griffith from Illinois. The Griffiths were invited by Flossie and Hugo Jackson.

Marvin and Ruth said they did not mind that we were not totally ready to receive guest. They felt so much at home that they worked with us by doing the mailings. Marvin enjoyed the "million dollar view" and the breeze. They were the perfect first guests. They stayed with us for a week and it was just like having family around.

Marvin sat on the balcony and read a lot and Ruth volunteered to help with the direct mail.

Marvin & Ruth Grffith and Flossie & Hugo Jackson

It was surreal. When they gave me the check to pay for their stay, I wanted to give it back! It did not seem right to take money for something I enjoyed giving away and had given away all of my life. It finally sunk in....this is now your business!!!

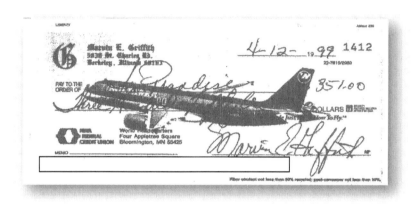

Copy of first check

They returned to Chicago and we kept in touch through Flossie. A couple of years later we got the news that Marvin had gone on to glory and that he never stopped talking about us and his stay at InnParadise.

Marvin has since gone to be with the Lord; but he and his wife will be forever remembered.

The Owner's Club …

In order to help introduce our inn to friends, family and others, we decided to create something called "The Owners Club."

License for The Owners' Club

We invited our church members and everyone we had come in contact with who had expressed an interest in coming to our inn once it was opened to join. For $200 they would be entitled to a three-night stay for no additional cost.

Additional nights were discounted 25% and the membership was non-transferable and valid for two years. Membership cards were issued. We had a total of 30 people to join. Many were able to come stay with us. The others supported the vision.

We also hired high school students to work with us on this and other projects.

Towards the end of my AT&T career, I worked in the Career Resource Center with a gentleman named, Dave Arterburn. During this time we became friends and I shared my dreams and hopes with him. Dave was very encouraging and supportive. He and his wife, Barbara, were one of the first members to join The Owners' Club.

It was a wonderful feeling to have them visit with us and for Dave to see my dream become a reality. They came to InnParadise several times and each time was truly a joy to be with them.

Dave and Barbara Arterburn, Suwanee GA

Well, June is now fast approaching and we have just about exhausted our reserve fund. We are ready for guest and already have a few bookings. This was another opportunity for God to do his thing.

After Paula retired, she was expecting to receive a lump sum payment from AT&T. She needed to respond to this offer by a certain date. With moving to St. Croix and having mail directed first to one address and then another, Paula did not receive this notice until it was too late to respond. She went through an appeals process but was denied. My advice to her was to let it go and continue on the course we were on. Paula was eventually able to "let go and let God."

In April of 1999, Paula receive a letter detailing a class action suit filed against AT&T and that she was included as a plaintiff and she could opt out if she wished. She remained a party in the suit and in June, she received her portion of the award, which was almost the exact amount she had been entitled to. A miracle, I'd say!

Our reserve fund is now in tack and we are ready for guests. Thank God, because our schedule was about to be altered. First, the lawyer for the estate responsible for correcting the deed moved back to Texas with no resolution to the case.

Our petition for rezoning was moving at a snails pace (typical for the island we would learn). Our six-month agreement with the estate was about to end and we had invested well over $40,000 so far. We extended our agreement with the estate, they got another lawyer, and we just continued in faith.

The Daily News, Saturday, February 19, 2000

Virgin Islands

PNR approves request to enlarge inn

By EUNICE BEDMINSTER
Daily News Staff

ST. CROIX — The Planning and Natural Resources Department has given an initial nod of approval to allow the owners of Innparadise to add more rooms to their bed-and-breakfast establishment. That does not sit well with some local homeowners who were slow in voicing their opposition and may now have to bite the bullet.

The request for a zoning variance by Tommie and Paula Broadnax was one of several that came Thursday before the Senate, sitting as the Committee of the Whole for a zoning hearing. Other applications included a request to allow a nursery school and bookstore at Sunny Isle Baptist Church and a request by Joseph Greenaway for a retail plumbing store and office in Estate Whim.

The Broadnaxes applied for a zoning variance to increase their four-room inn to nine rooms. PNR officials earlier had approved the request, saying that despite notices to homeowners in the vicinity, there had been no response for or against the change.

But on Thursday night Richard Borck, who said he was president of the Homeowners Association — representing 45 homeowners at Little Princess Hill, where the inn is located — presented a petition to the Committee of the Whole in opposition to the proposed zoning change.

Borck said that while homeowners had no problems with the inn as is, they feared an increase in rooms would increase traffic in the area and cause wear and tear on the narrow road maintained by homeowners through association

dues. Borck said that homeowners were also against the Broadnaxes' request because they feared it would devalue their property.

Attorney Richard Austin, who testified in support of the zoning variance, said that the inn would mean a small boost to St. Croix in that more rooms would mean increased tourist traffic. He praised Tommie Broadnax, a contractor, and his wife, Paula, for her design skills, in turning the once four-bedroom home into a beautiful inn overlooking picturesque downtown Christiansted and the Caribbean Sea.

"The Broadnaxes' house has already increased in value to about a third" of the cost, Austin said. "If these people would stop and visit the Broadnaxes, I guarantee you that after one visit they would go and take their name off the petition."

Tommie Broadnax testified that the improvements to the inn were necessary to stay in business.

"Economically, we could not make an even break or make money from four rooms, so we need to expand," he said. Broadnax has proposed a two-story structure with a breezeway connecting it to the existing building.

Senate President Vargrave Richards cautioned those present that requests given an initial nod by PNR are usually approved by the Legislature and those denied by PNR are usually turned down. In addition to Richards, only three other senators were present — Almando "Rocky" Liburd, Norman Jn Baptiste and Ann Golden.

The zoning requests next go before the full Senate.

They include:

• Maria Calderon (authorized agent for Jose Calderon) — request for amendment of Official Zoning Map SCZ-20 for Plots 151-152, Estate Richmond, Company Quarter, St. Croix from R-3 (Residential - Medium Density) to B-3 (Business - Scattered) to operate a commercial warehouse.

• Beverly Collins — Request for amendment of Official Zoning Map SCZ-20 for Plot no. 10, Estate Tipperary, East End Quarter, St Croix, from R-2 (Residential- Low Density One and Two Family) to B-3 (Business -Scattered) to allow commercial use of a well on the property.

• Vilma Danois — request for amendment of Official Zone Map SCZ-6 for Plot no. 88-D, Estate La Grande Princess, Company Quarter, St. Croix, from R-2 (Residential-Low Density One and Two Family) to B-3 (Business - Scattered).

• Sunny Isle Baptist Church — request for amendment of Official Zoning Map SCZ-12 for Plot no. 2, Estate Caldwell, Queen Quarter, St. Croix, from C (Commercial) to B-3 (Business- Scattered) to allow a nursery school, bookstore and residential uses.

• Joseph Greenaway — request for amendment of Official Zoning Map SCZ-10 for Plot no. 78-H, Estate Whim, West End Quarter, St. Croix, from R-2 (Residential - Low Density One and Two Family) to B-3 (Business - Scattered) to allow a retail plumbing supply store and office.

• Paul Horsford — request for amendment of Official Zoning Map SCZ-6 for Plot no. 9-G, Estate Constitution Hill, Queen's Quarter, St. Croix, from R-1 (Residential-Low Density) to R-2 (Residential -Low Density One and Two Family).

Sister, Janice, Ma Mildred, Tommie and me

A very special guest...

Tommie and I were always very excited when family members were able to come visit us. We wanted all of them to see the blessing that had been bestowed upon us. My mother had made it clear that she was not flying across all of that water! So when elderly guests arrived, it was a special time to me.

Janice, Tommie's sister, was the caregiver to his mother. Ma Mildred had some health challenges; but made it clear to Janice that she wanted to come see where her son was. Upon planning to come, they found out that the St. Croix hospital could not accommodate her with the dialysis treatments she required. It was determined that the only alternative would be for her to go to St. Thomas three days of her week long vacation for the treatments.

Being the trooper that she was, that was fine with her. The trips to St. Thomas became a part of her vacation experience. Tommie arranged to take her via seaplane those days and she had a ball being with her son and flying on the seaplane.

We are so grateful that Janice could bring her and that Ma Mildred was able to have those experiences before being called home to glory.

CHAPTER 9

THE MISSING LINK FOUND

After a few years of marriage, it was very evident to me that Tommie's life experiences (to this point) had prepared him to be my helpmeet! Just about every job he had previously held allowed him to do most of the projects required for us to create our bed and breakfast inn.

With over 30 years of carpentry and home repair experience, Tommie did primarily all of the renovations and remodeling for our inn; including, adding bathrooms to each room, laying tile; adding decks which allowed each guest direct access to the seaside view; building our dining room table and buffet and much, much more. As you know, when you have a property it must be maintained. Yes, Tommie was the maintenance man, as well!

In his earlier years, Tommie managed several fast food restaurants like McDonalds, Roy Rogers and Dairy Queen. He acquired skills in food preparation, payroll, and personnel and, of course, customer service. All of these skills were critical to the success of our business.

One of Tommie's friends owned a printing business. Tommie worked primarily in marketing and sales. It was so much fun to create and design all of our marketing materials. He created our logo which was used on all materials, including: brochures, business cards, and any printed material and even our own InnParadise flag.

And last, but not least....during a lag in his construction business, Tommie returned to school to become a phlebotomist. He drew blood for hospitals and insurance companies. When I was going through my cancer treatments, he nursed me back to good health. One of the memorable times is when my port got infected and had to be packed. The bandages had to be changed frequently. I could not look at the hole in my chest; but he had no problem and lovingly did so. I jokingly tell him that I think he wanted to be a doctor and got his license from television.

Mama used to say…. "That Tommie uses his head for more than just a hat rack!" Her way of saying that he's a smart man! And I agree! Tommie was my missing link!

Tommie, my missing link

CHAPTER 10

IT PAYS TO PROMOTE YOURSELF

During my career, I spent 18 years in Marketing. During that time I learned how to promote myself. Upon retirement, I began receiving the AT&T Retirement Publication. As I read the publication, I said to myself, "Wow! I would love to be on the cover of this magazine because I have a story to tell."

I wrote to AT&T's Public Relations Department and asked if they would be interested in doing an interview with me. They said definitely!

AT&T sent a writer, Martha Hickson, and a photographer to document our story. Tommie and I felt like celebrities. We were interviewed, followed during our day-to-day duties, and photographed. They also joined us at events….even church service.

AT&T publishes article in Encore Magazine Summer of 2000:

Paradise found

"We wanted to manage the business; we didn't want the business to manage us," says Tommie, who takes time with Paula every day to enjoy St. Croix's tropical beauty.

encore 16

Paula Smith Broadnax

Third and fourth quarters 2000

spotlight

Martha Hickson

Paula and Tommie Broadnax open their tropical dream house to guests from around the world

Open the door to Paula and Tommie Broadnax's home in St. Croix, and your jaw will drop as you're drawn to the panoramic window with a sweeping view of the Caribbean's shimmering, turquoise waters, seaplanes landing in the harbor and sailboats gliding along the horizon.

For visitors to "innparadise," as the Broadnaxes named their bed-and-breakfast (B&B) and home, that view is proof that a Virgin Islands vacation has begun. But for Paula and Tommie, it's evidence of a dream come true.

The dream began in 1994, when the thought of running an inn popped into Paula's head. "I don't know where the idea came from; I had never even stayed at an inn," says Paula, who retired from AT&T in 1998 as a Human Resources career-resources manager. "But for as long as I can remember, my home has been a haven for family members, friends and strangers."

Living in Atlanta, a single mother of two grown children, Paula began exploring innkeeping. She completed a course on managing a B&B at Oglethorpe University in Atlanta, stayed at inns whenever she traveled, and even used the idea as a case study for her AT&T-sponsored project-management training.

Then in November 1995, Paula met Tommie, also single after raising two children. They began dating, and Paula shared her dream. "I was ready to pack up my tools and move," says Tommie, who had owned a carpentry business since his career as an air-traffic controller ended during a 1980 strike.

The couple married in May 1996 and soon received devastating news: Paula had breast cancer. But illness only fueled Paula's passion. "I realized life was short," she says. "If I wanted an inn, I had to do it now."

Sources of "inn-spiration"

So Paula and Tommie picked up the pace on their innkeeping education. They attended a seminar in Cape May, N.J., the B&B capital of the East Coast. They learned tricks of the trade from seasoned innkeepers. And wherever they went, they told people about their dream.

"Everybody said, 'Good for you; let us know when you're open,'" Paula says. "Those words were really powerful."

As their confidence grew, Paula and Tommie began scouting locations. "I knew I wanted to be in the Caribbean," Paula says. "I've always loved the islands. The water is so peaceful and healing."

So, taking their friends' advice, the Broadnaxes visited St. Croix, the largest of the U.S. Virgin Islands. "We loved what we saw – the rolling hills, the space, the people," Tommie says.

When Paula accepted a retirement package from AT&T in 1998, the next step was clear. The couple moved that summer to St. Croix, rented a condo and searched for the ideal property. They considered buying an existing inn, but nothing

continued on next page

"We really work well together in the kitchen," says Paula, here preparing breakfast. "When Tommie lays down a spoon, I'll pick it up. We don't even have to say a word."

The inn's cozy common room and its spectacular view reflect Paula's innkeeping philosophy: "You're not coming to an inn; you're not coming to a hotel. You're guests in our home."

17 *encore*

82

Third and fourth
quarters 2000

spotlight

Paradise *found*

continued from previous page

struck their fancy until Tommie spotted an ad in a local real estate magazine.

"We drove up the hill and saw a long, low building that looked like a lodge," Tommie says of his first glimpse of the 30-year-old private home that would become innparadise. "As soon as we walked in the door and saw the view, there was no question. This was it."

Paula and Tommie closed on the house that winter, and welcomed their first guest the following April after investing months of sweat equity. "We're still sweating!" Paula jokes.

Tommie remodeled bedrooms, built bathrooms, laid tile and constructed the bar and dining table. It's no wonder Paula calls innparadise "the house that Tommie built."

Meanwhile, Paula launched a direct-mail campaign to the more than 3,000 friends, church members and others whose names she had collected over the years.

So far, innparadise has welcomed visitors from throughout the United States, England and Denmark. "Our guests open the world to us," Tommie says. "They come from different places, have different experiences, and we get to share in that."

When those guests arrive, they stay in one of four rooms Paula has decorated in a style she describes as "light, airy and colorful with a Caribbean flair."

Advice from the innkeepers

If you've ever thought about running a bed-and-breakfast, Paula and Tommie Broadnax offer these tips.

- Assess yourself: Paula recommends reading "So You Want to Be an Innkeeper" from Chronicle Books to understand whether you have what it takes.

- Practice innkeeping: Stay at inns; talk to professional innkeepers. Some might even let you help out for a weekend. "It's always good to surround yourself with people doing what you want to do," Tommie says. "Visiting other inns gave us tips on how to prepare food quickly."

- Join an association: Paula and Tommie are members of the Professional Association of Innkeepers International (http://www.paii.org) and the African American Association of Innkeepers International (http://www.africanamericaninns.com/). Each offers aspiring-innkeeper memberships. "Those associations open the door to resources and people who can support you as you move forward," Paula says.

- Market yourself: "Once you decide you're serious, begin marketing immediately. Tell people what you're doing and start building a mailing list," Paula says. "Bring your business cards wherever you go."

- Be a guest at your own inn: "Before we opened innparadise, we stayed in each room as if we were guests to determine if there was anything uncomfortable," Tommie says. "You'll learn things your guests might not tell you."

"There is no way this dream could have been realized without God sending Tommie to me," Paula says.

"This job is easy because we're doing what we like to do," says Tommie, who believes the attention to detail he learned as an air-traffic controller helps him keep the inn running smoothly.

Paula Smith Broadnax

spotlight

Steel drums and cheese grits

A typical day at innparadise begins in the common room facing the tropical breezes and sunshine. With a recording of steel drums playing softly in the background, Paula and Tommie serve a Southern-style breakfast they've prepared together. One morning, guests might dine on banana pancakes and spiced peaches; on another, the menu could include an omelet with cheese grits and biscuits.

From innparadise, visitors can take a short drive to the island's many attractions, including white-sand beaches; the capital city, Christiansted; and the underwater snorkel trail at Buck Island National Monument.

Afterward, they can try linin', the island term for relaxing. In the late afternoon, visitors might find Paula and Tommie doing just that on the inn's deck set amid a glorious display of pink and pur-

ple flowers. The only sign of a fast-paced life: the neon-green geckos that dart from branch to branch.

According to guest Pam Mitchell of Decatur, Ga., "Innparadise is an atmosphere for relaxation – so wonderful and serene I could stay here forever."

Although innparadise seems perfect as it is, Paula and Tommie have big plans for its future. Between Paula's occasional "off island" trips to the mainland for medical treatments, the couple plan to expand the inn to 10 guest rooms, open a restaurant and gift shop, and convert a hallway into a gallery of local art. "There are a lot of possibilities with this property," Tommie says.

But no matter how big or broad their business interests grow, Paula and Tommie will live by the same simple philosophy that's brought them success: "You may arrive a stranger, but we want you to leave as part of the family." 🅴

A special inn-vitation to *Encore* readers

Paula and Tommie Broadnax invite all readers to visit innparadise. When you book a reservation for four or more nights, just mention *Encore* and you'll receive a 25 percent discount and an island tour for two (valid Oct. 2000 through April 2001). To contact innparadise, call **340-713-9803** or e-mail **innparadise@worldnet.att.net** Visit innparadise online at **http://www.innparadisestcroix.com**

The article was awesome....we were the first African American cover that I am aware of. It was distributed to retirees around the world! People emailed, called and even visited as a result of the exposure. They would be on cruises with St. Croix as a port stop and come by to say hello.

One very memorable story is of a lady diagnosed with cancer who had received the publication (her husband was an AT&T retiree). Upon reading it she told him that one day she wanted to visit us and she put the article away. Several years later they came....what a joy that was! We had an awesome visit.

She had just completed chemo and the vacation was very refreshing and healing for her. A few years later, we were informed that she had passed away. I am so glad that I met her and that she had the opportunity to come visit us.

Paula Smith Broadnax

A freelance writer found our info online and included us in this
article.

excursions

Getaway
Destinations

Four Seasons Resort in Mexico

by Kimberlyn Griffin

Stressed out? Beat down? Looking for an excuse to get away from the pressures of work and the demands of home life? Look, no further. Here's your chance to escape to a luxury resort or hotel in paradise.

In this real life fantasy, you will get a taste of "the good life," while visiting one of our five getaway destinations, complete with features to soothe your mind and ease your soul.

Innparadise Bed & Breakfast in St. Croix

A "home away from home," without the responsibilities, is what you will enjoy most about this cozy, private bed and breakfast inn. Innparadise, an African-American-owned bed and breakfast, is located just minutes from Christiansted, and sits on a hillside just overlooking the beautiful Caribbean Sea. For more information, call (340) 713-7803 or email Innparadise@worldnet.att.net

UPSCALE DECEMBER/JANUARY 2000

106

86

African-Americans do not generally seek the bed and breakfast experience. Staying at a bed and breakfast inn provides a setting which allows guests to get to know one another. Guests also have the advantage of onsite concierge service.

Business Monday

Monday, May 17, 1999 ▼ Page 22

Tom and Paula Broadnax pose in the sitting room of their new bed and breakfast, Innparadise. The couple are living their dream of owning and operating an inn on St. Croix.

Daily News Photos by GARY McCRACKEN

St. Croix B&B targets traveling African-Americans

Splash of Southern hospitality includes comforts of home

87

Paula Smith Broadnax

The following article was written by Dennis Mccluster, a local newspaper reporter. As God would have it, his family was a member of Greenforest Community Baptist Church, our Atlanta church. His mom taught my sons in Sunday School.

Some of Tommie and my design work. This is a brochure of the inn which we created.

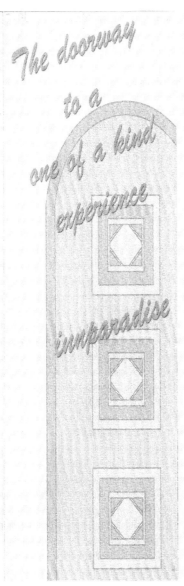

innparadise

The sensational view is just the beginning. Once you walk through the door, you will instantly feel at home. Tommie and Paula will embrace you with their southern hospitality ... right here in the Caribbean.

The convenient location, peaceful environment, breathtaking views and homey atmosphere make our inn ideal for business travelers and vacationers alike.

Our common area is as spacious as it is cozy. The open area overlooks an expansive view of the Caribbean Sea and Christiansted Harbor. The comfy seating area and beautifully designed bar call for lounging and relaxation.

Just beyond the common area is intimate dining. The menu of savory southern dishes and lively conversations are the main ingredients for a memorable experience. Our dining area has quickly become a popular place for mingling with the hosts and other guests. We credit this area for being the origin of many life-long friendships.

The bright and cheerful rooms are an absolute delight. The tropical color palette and sea views are constant reminders that you are in the Caribbean. Each of our five newly remodeled rooms is uniquely different and equipped with many amenities.

The serenity and beauty of *innparadise* will warm your soul, refresh your mind and liven your spirit. Join Tommie and Paula for a one of a kind experience in paradise.

innparadise

a bed & breakfast inn

innparadise

a bed & breakfast inn

St. Croix, U.S. Virgin Islands

Located on a quiet, semi-secluded road. Convenient to Christiansted town, nearby beaches, restaurants and more. Spectacular harbor view. Five newly remodeled rooms equipped with many amenities including complimentary beverage bar and free internet access. Ours is a smoke-free environment. Join us... *innparadise!*

Southern Hospitality in the Caribbean

Telephone: 340 713 9803
Toll free: 866 800 9803
Fax: 340 713 8722
Website: www.innparadisestcroix.com
Email: info@innparadisestcroix.com

Photos and Design by Debbie Sun

A view from the Inn

Paula Smith Broadnax

Tommie and I were active members of the Small Inns of St. Croix. Paula was the Marketing chairperson.

In May 2000, Tommie traveled to the states to help his brother renovate his basement. I remained on the island to receive the many guests scheduled to arrive.

With Agatha, our housekeeper and Mr. Johnson, the gardener, it was not a difficult task. They were so proud of us and treated the business like they owned it. The Inn always sparkled and the lawn and tropical plants were beautiful.

Agatha

Mr. Johnson

Charlene and Herbert (from Atlanta and our home church) came to the inn in May 2000. It was wonderful to see them for many reasons. One of which is that Charlene and I were a part of an eldercare support group at AT&T. She and I had a lot in common as caregivers to our elderly mothers.

During their visit, I received a call from my eldest brother, William, with whom my mother was now residing in Chicago. I never will forget this words....Mama, is gone! Mama, is gone! I said, she is gone where?? Then, I knew. All I could do is scream NO, NO, NO!!!! She had died of heart failure as she was being taken to the doctor for a routine checkup.

I was distraught! Thank God that Herbert and Charlene were there to console me. It did not take long for word to travel around the island and within the hour people were coming by and calling to check on me because many knew that Tommie was off island.

I thank God for allowing my mother to live for 83 years. She was and IS so special to me! I am so grateful that she lived with me for many years and I was able to show her how much I loved her.

Bessie Lee Smith

Our dear friend Bonnie volunteered to inn sit as I made arrangements to return to the states to Mama's homegoing services.

Bonnie and friends

CHAPTER 11

September 11, 2001

Paula's 9/11 experience ...

On this dreadful day, I can close my eyes and remember it like it was yesterday! I had completed chemo and radiation; however, I was still under the doctor's care and returned to the states for follow-up visits with my breast surgeon, Dr. Rogsbert Phillips-Reed.

I was in the waiting room. The television was on and there were only a few of us in the room. Initially, we were not paying close attention to the television; however, when BREAKING NEWS came across the screen, it got our attention. As I stared at the screen, I could not believe what I was seeing! It all appeared to be something that would be in a movie. I was in shock!

My visit with the doctor went well and she was pleased with my progress.

I returned to my "play" sister, Barbara's home where I called my husband to see if he was watching the news. Of course, he was! I told him that I would see him soon because I was scheduled to return in time for my birthday on September 14. Needless to say, flights were cancelled and my travel plans were changed.

I was ready to go home and became anxious because I really did not want to fly back to St. Croix; but we all know that I had no choice but to fly.

In the meantime, my family and friends decided that they would give me a birthday party. It was held at my sister Sharon's home. My children, family and a host of friends came to help me celebrate. It was a wonderful time and I am grateful that they wanted to create the occasion for me.

Paula and Barbara

When airlines were finally re-opened, I planned my return trip. The flight back to St. Croix was eerie in a way. There was much silence. Not much chatter. I know I was quietly praying and thinking about what had happened days prior. Needless to say, I was so thankful to cross the water and land safely on St. Croix and to be with my husband. Everything had changed!

Tommie's 9/11 experience ...

From June to November (which is off season for tourism) things can get pretty slow. Being a home repair contractor, work is usually not hard to find. I had started a job for one of our guest who had come to St. Croix to work at the hospital.

The doctor and his family had moved into a condo on the beach and needed some remodeling. On the morning of September 11, I had just started on the interior painting when his wife called me to look at what was happening on the news. As we gathered around the TV, they were just replaying the first plane hitting the north tower of the World Trade Center in New York.

I was stunned and surprised, as I am sure everyone in the world was. As a former air traffic controller, my first thought was that the plane must have had a total failure of its control system for the pilot to crash into the building. The approaches into JFK and LaGuardia would not normally take a plane close to the WTC.

Now we are totally absorbed by what is happening. The news persons are all speculating on what could have happened and a few moments later the second plane flew into the south tower. I think everyone now understood that this was an act of terrorism. The likelihood of a plane crashing into the WTC is remote but, for two planes to do so would have to be intentional.

I tried to call Paula on her cell phone (since she was off island at the time) but all the line where busy and remained so for most of that day.

We continued to watch the news as the towers fell and reports of another plane crashing into the Pentagon was broadcast. I had worked briefly at the Pentagon when I first got out of the Army and that connection made it that much harder to see the destruction that occurred. My thoughts also turned to the mornings I use to ride the PATH train from New Jersey into the city, getting off at the WTC, with thousands of other workers coming into the city.

I could not bring myself to continue working that day, so I returned to the Inn and resumed the vigil of watching the news. Then we heard about another plane over Pennsylvania and possibly heading for Washington, DC. That plane, as you know, crashed in a field in Pennsylvania, the last plane not accounted for.

Paula was scheduled to come back to the island that week; but she had to wait over a week to get a flight. I would suspect that almost everyone who had access to the news that day can remember what they were doing. I know that I will never forget.

CHAPTER 12

THE DREAM MANIFESTED

Well, I am here to tell you that dreams do come true! It was not an easy journey, but I can truly say that every step, trial, and encounter was worth it. I knew that we were moving forward towards the fulfillment of what we had set out to do. Tommie and I worked from the time we acquired the property until we left St. Croix.

Numerous hours of "sweat equity" (mainly, Tommie's) went into creating what we hoped would be a beautiful and serene environment where our guests would leave feeling refreshed and renewed.

The fact we were blessed to be able to create our inn from "nothing" has been an exceptional experience. Let us present to you……. InnParadise.

The Million Dollar View

innparadise
a bed & breakfast inn

"Southern hospitality in the Caribbean"
A spectacular sea view

(340) 713 - 9803 or toll free (866) 800 - 9803

Yes, three flags …..U.S. flag, Virgin Islands flag, and of course, an InnParadise flag (designed and made by Tommie, of course!)

The following pages show rooms in InnParadise guest rooms.   Each room was given the name (as listed).   Some names were taken from estate names on the island.

Paula's Fancy

Peaches 'n Cream

Seaside Retreat

Contentment

Kathryn's Hope

CHAPTER 13

SOME OF OUR MEMORABLE GUESTS

In order to track where our guests were from, we placed a world map on the wall and placed push pins in the places they came from.

Our guests came from 37 of the 50 U.S. States; U. S. Virgin Islands, Puerto Rico and Guam; and places including: Israel, United Kingdom, Denmark, Canada, Netherlands, Tortola, Anguilla, Trinidad, Barbados, French Guyana, St. Lucia, St. Vincent, Antigua, and St. Maarten. We were an international inn indeed!

This was the most joyous part of owning the inn……having the world come to our door. The chance to meet new people, learn about their culture and share ourselves (especially at mealtime) was what we lived for. Many a people tried grits for the first time and loved them.   Tommie's banana rum pancakes were also a hit.

Many of our guests attended church with us as a part of their vacation experience. Some felt so much at home that they cooked for us! We told our guests that we wanted to help create a memorable visit with us and we did everything we could to make it happen.

Naita and her daughter, Quiana visited us from California to celebrate Quiana's 18th birthday. To help make this a memorable event, we planned a beach party for Quiana and invited our beach group to help us make it memorable. Quiana was introduced to local foods, music and island hospitality.

Our beach group consists of between 30-40 locals and transplants from the states who got together on holidays (and any other opportunity to go to the beach, lime or relax, eat and just have fun. Needless to say….they rose to the occasion and Quiana thanked us for a birthday she will never forget.

Some of the Beach Group

A bond was formed between us….so tight that Naita returned to island on two occasions to "inn sit" for us (once while we attended an inn keeping seminar and again when we took a vacation to London, England). She loved her island experiences so much, that she relocated to St. Croix. Naita is now lovingly known as my "sistah." She also volunteered to be our property manager when we returned to the states in November 2003.

Quiana and her mother, Naita

Our inn ... a refuge

One of our friends encountered a lady at the beach who seemed quite troubled. When he approached her, he determined she was considering committing suicide. He was able to calm her but needed to find a place for her to go because her issues were with her family. He brought her to the inn and asked if she could spend the night. We put her up.

The next morning we invited her to breakfast. The guests included a couple from England and they were aware of what had occurred. The lady felt comfortable enough to share with the guests and us. She left, but later came back to thank us and tell us how she had drawn strength from us that morning. To God be the glory!

It's your birthday …

Aunt Daisy is the elderly Panamanian aunt of our "sistah" Naita. She came to visit Naita for a few weeks and I was asked if Aunt Daisy could stay at the inn with me a few days while Naita worked. She was great company for me and very entertaining and enlightening. We talked a lot, cooked West Indian food and toured the island.

Tommie and I had planned a fellowship for the Men's Bible study group and their spouses. Naita and Aunt Daisy were invited to join us. During the party Aunt Daisy wanted to propose a toast. She said "I want to thank all of you nice people for coming out to help me celebrate my 81st birthday." Tommie and I looked at Naita with a question mark on our faces.

Aunt Daisy went on to say that everything was beautiful and that she would always remember this special day. We began to cheer and congratulate her and went on to celebrate Aunt Daisy's birthday with great fanfare!

From our Guests …

We placed journals in each of the rooms and invited our guests to share some of the highlights of their visit to paradise.

Following are a few excerpts of their entries:

Thank you for your warmth and hospitality! You truly own a piece of paradise! You made us feel at home. In fact, one evening I said to Barry "It's time to go home." It didn't occur to me to say 'to our accommodations.'

Leonie & Barry
Canada

Sharing your "home" has been one of the greatest privileges and pleasures I've known. I'm so thankful to our Father that we are related and that we know we are now each other's keeper.

Betty
Georgia

"InnParadise"… your home is aptly named. It is paradise on earth, with your spirit, hospitality and warmth of love that is so infectious. Thank you for sharing this and much more. The scenery from all of the rooms is breathtaking.

Jan and Carol
England

I feel that you bring a spirituality to this place which make people feel good and become infused with your loving, caring spirits.

Edna
Connecticut

The blend of absolute joy and grief experienced at our wonderful home will continue to bless me for the rest of my life. Thank you for the love and comfort shown to me at my mother's death yesterday. What better place for this to happen! I will remember this always. Your warm hearts showed me that the service you extend is your ministry. You are really a blessing to the world.

Marjorie
Jamaica

Thank you just doesn't say it; but that's as close as I can come for such a wonderful visit.

Alex & Tracey
Maryland

I love you. I had a beautiful time. Thank you!

Ma Mildred (Tommie's mother)
Maryland

I stayed here a month. I saw many people come and go and everyone seemed to have the same feeling I had. This place is a bit of heaven on earth! Words cannot truly express how I feel for you both but saying I love you is my heart talking. You were my strength when I needed it and my ears when I needed those. God bless you both!

Tammie
Florida

You two make InnParadise truly paradise by being the perfect host and hostess. Thank you for making my stay here so pleasant, though it was short. I plan to return so my son can stay here with me and I can beat you at Scrabble!

Kathleen

Utah

Thank you for leaving the lights on for me. I truly enjoyed my stay at InnParadise. This was my first time staying at a bed & breakfast and you surely have set the bar high as far as what to expect from such an establishment!

Catherine

Michigan

As a return guest, I appreciate your "hominess". I feel like family. This is definitely my home away from home.

Patricia

St. Thomas, VI

Love is in everything you do. InnParadise is a respite for the body and the soul. Thank you for your generosity and for making "your home, my home"

Leslie

Indiana

Thank you. Staying here has been a pleasure. You both are the most charming and generous people I have ever met! I hope all of your dreams continue to come true.

Stephanie

Conneticut

One of many thank you cards:

All of our guests were special and memorable. I would like to introduce you to a few of them.

Triathletes

St. Croix was the host site for the pre-qualifiers to the Hawaiian Ironman competition. Athletes came from all over the world for this event. For several years our inn was filled with the activities of housing and helping the athletes prepare to compete. The day before the event, they usually returned to the inn after training and began to fill their bodies with carbs! The route of the runners came down the road in front of the inn. We would rise early in the morning and go down the hill to the road to cheer our guests and friends on to victory.

Tracy and Alex

A dance group came to the island for annual competitions. The event was held under a huge tent, down the hill from us at Condo Row. We could stand on our balcony and see the participants and hear the great music as they danced.

Our guest, Tracy, was a dancer and she invited us to come down and join them. We had a blast learning the steps and dancing with the group.

The following year both Tracy and her fiancée stayed with us and the year after that they got married on the island and the entire wedding party was with us. It was a great time getting to know both families. We attended the wedding. It was a beautiful seaside wedding on the beach where the dance teams had performed year after year.

Tracy and Alex were web designers and since they come to St. Croix each year, we struck a barter deal with them. For the redesign and hosting of our website, we offered free accommodations to them when they visited St. Croix for their dance competition.

Roger W. Morgan and family ...

Roger was a disc jockey from out West. His sister-in-law Wookeum, had been diagnosed with cancer and the family thought it would be great for her to get away to a healing environment. They chose St. Croix and were our guests. During the time of their visit, my brother, his wife, mother-in-law and daughter were visiting. An immediate family connection was made by all of the guests.

Roger and his wife, Kangja encouraged us to take time to go sailing and snorkeling with them at Buck Island. Wookeum and Jason (her friends) took over running the inn and checked in other expectant guests.

The Morgans and Broadnaxes

Our guests taking us out to dinner

a BIG hug for Roger!!!

My brother, Rev. W. H. Foster Sr., was scheduled to preach at Pastor Richard Austin's church. We invited Roger and his family to join us and were delighted that they accepted.

Rev. Foster was born in the south and has been in Chicago for many years. His sermon on that day will be forever remembered. It was entitled "That's What Friends are For" from Mark 2:1-12. William (as we call him) said that he was very impressed by the friends we had made while on the island and how they had accepted and supported us and our business.

Our friends continually embraced our guests. They took it upon themselves to make sure guests had a wonderful and memorable visit to the island. Our friends had beach parties, gave tours of the island, invited our guests to their homes, and showed them other acts of kindnesses.

The sermon was about a lame man who had been taken to see Jesus for a healing by his friends. His friends had taken him up on the roof and lowered him down at the feet of Jesus because they loved him and wanted him to be healed....Rev. Foster concluded "That's What Friends are For." It was a very moving sermon and it gave us all something to think about.

Sunday Service

The following year we received word that Wookeum had passed away.   Roger and the family were returning to St. Croix for a Memorial Service. They booked their rooms with us and asked us to be a part of the service. We went to a special spot at Point Udall (the eastern most point of the United States) and scattered Wookeum's ashes upon the Sea. That is what she wanted.

Roger and his wife had been considering relocating to the island following their first visit and were moved to go forward with their plans. They became residents of St. Croix.

William Chapman Nyaho, Concert Pianist

The St. Croix Landmark Society holds annual events at Whim Plantation. Tommie and I attended an event and heard a very talented concert pianist perform who was originally from Africa. I was very impressed and thought it would be great to introduce him to our church congregation and the youth at our church.

So, following his performance, we waited until he had greeted everyone, introduced ourselves and invited him to join us at church on Sunday. He accepted! We went to his hotel and picked him up for service.

He played a classical number which was beautiful; but did not seem to be well received. For his second selection he did another classical number, but it was from an original Caribbean song, which the congregation was familiar with. This got a rousing response!

We invited him to join us at the inn for brunch so that we would get to know him better. The following year he stayed at our inn.

Upon his return he informed us that he had a spiritual connection with St. Croix. When he viewed the slave records at Whim Plantation, he saw the name of his mother...which was quite unusual!

Spiritual Blessings ...

Romans 10:15

And how are they to preach unless they are sent? As it is written, "How beautiful are the feet of those who preach the good news!"

My desire had been (and is) to seek God's guidance and wisdom as I moved to make my dream a reality. I know that wisdom is found in His Word (the Bible) and through prayer.

Our inn became a special place of healing. When you entered and looked out at the sea, you could feel and see the awesome power of God. Many who entered our doors were compelled to openly pray for us and the surroundings in which they had found themselves.

They included:

The Church Planting Team of the Southern Baptist Convention - Southeastern Region. (Rev. Joshua Smith; Rev. Dennis [and Pam] Mitchell and Rev. Kenneth Weathersby).

Bishop Claude Willie, Rev. Michael Bell and Rev. Carlton Brown of the Annual AME Zion Church Convention.

The Church ladies from St. Thomas, USVI who left came for church meeting. Upon their departure, I began to clean the inn. I found the door knobs to be slippery. When I went to our vehicle, I saw a cross marked on the dusty signage. It was then I realized that they had anointed the place with oil.

Dr. Dorothy Neville (from The Institute of Healing in Anguilla) who helped us realize that "We were the inn...not the building!!"

Once is not enough ...

To get away from the cold winters in Grand Forks, ND, Lois would spend two weeks at InnParadise Bed and Breakfast Inn. Inns are a great place to stay for those traveling alone.

Lois would stay with us for years. One year, she brought a friend, Alma, who became very ill. Alma had to be airlifted to Puerto Rico for medical care. We are delighted to report that she recovered.

Lois was very interesting, knowledgeable, and adventurous. She snorkeled for the first time while visiting us.

Lois Hukom

Lois and Alma

Family is very important to us. We are so grateful that the following family members were able to come see how God had blessed us.

Family Comes to the Island …

Son, Darryl, and wife, Frances

TaKuma and Sharon, Sister

NiAya, niece

Paula Smith Broadnax

Granddaughter, Alaysia and Daughter, Tia

Barbara, Ms. Letba, William and Louise
(Brother and family)

Our "family" – The Austins, Andersons and us, Broadnaxes

CHAPTER 14

OUR COMMUNITY FAMILY

Since the time I was a teenager, I can remember being in a choir. I have always loved to sing….even though my youngest brother says that I can't! So when I was invited to join the island choir…I jumped at the opportunity. It was comprised of locals and transplants from the states.

We sang all over the island. Tommie and I offered to host rehearsals at the inn when we did not have guests. Those times were beautiful. To hear the music flowing through the inn and up the hill was awesome! The group was very talented. We even recorded a CD!!

Being a cancer survivor and wanting to give back to the community, I got involved with a Cancer Support Group on the island. I participated in Relay for Life and the inn was made available for support group meetings. Many lasting friendships were formed and continue today.

Men's Bible Study was also held at the inn until we left the island.

We were involved in many community events. One of which was an Arts Festival brought to the island by Madeline McCray. As a financial supporter of the event, we were given tickets to the all events which included a dialogue by Danny Glover, Glynn Turman and Sonia Sanchez. We also attended poetry reading by Ms. Sanchez.

I was scheduled to leave the island so Tommie planned a "going away" party for me, inviting our beach friends and others. We extended the invitation to Danny Glover and his entourage and they accepted. It was a blast! Music, card games, barbecue, and all the trimmings for a wonderful gathering. Our special guests were like our newly introduced "cousins." Our friends talked about this for a long time!

PERFORMING ARTS FESTIVAL
YOUR FAVORITE CELEBRITIES
A CULTURAL EXCHANGE EXPERIENCE

Surrounded by the beautiful blue-green Caribbean sea and white sandy beaches.
On St. Croix in the United States Virgin Islands: July 4th - 7th 2002.

Greetings Friend,

Do you remember where you were the week of July 4th - 8th, 2000? I was watching a dream materialize as guest by fabulous guest arrived to participate in the inaugural St. Croix Center Stage Performing Arts Festival in the United States Virgin Islands. As actors, and festival co-chairpersons Janet DuBois and John Amos entered the airport I asked myself: "self, why are you so lucky?" The answer came swiftly: "you aren't lucky, you're blessed."

That thought brought a smile to my lips because it was too true. How else could I possibly explain the presence of world-renowned poet Sonia Sanchez or Tony Award winning actress and St. Croix Center Stage's guest of honor Virginia Capers, on island to celebrate her 50th year anniversary in the entertainment industry. How could I explain all the other wonderful, talented

Virginia Capers & Glynn Turman Festival Co-chairs July 2002

artists like Glynn Turman, Dick Anthony Williams, Sheryl Lee-Ralph, Jeffrey Anderson-Gunter, *All My Children's* Cameron Mathison, Matthew St. Patrick. What about producer, director Woodie King, Jr. or director Seret Scott? Imagine the Off-Broadway play *Shades of Harlem*, the entire magnificent cast here on

John Amos & Janet DuBois Festival Co-chairs July 2000

our little island to upset our sweet mangoes with all that tappin! How could I explain this? Luck? Methinks not.

No one person with a thimble of luck could ever lay sole claim to the success of an event of this kind. The credit belongs to all the dedicated individuals who worked so hard volunteering their time and energy to help create something special. The credit belongs to sponsors such as American Airlines, the USVI Department of Tourism, Hovensa Oil Refinery, Sunny Isle Shopping Center, Vitel Cellular, Caribbean Broadcast Union

JULY 2001

Largest of the three US Virgin Islands, 28 miles long and 7 miles wide, St. Croix is one of the most beautiful resort areas in the Caribbean.

A variety of landscapes from dry cacti-covered areas to a dense rain forest surrounded by rolling hills and white sandy beaches. • When you attend the next St. Croix Center Stage Performing Arts Festival July 4th - 7th, 2002, you can go horseback riding, scuba diving, kayaking, parasailing, windsurfing, hiking, play tennis, golf, do a little gambling, or go to a spa. • You can visit historic sites such as: Whim Great House Museum, the Heritage Trail, or the forts in Christiansted and *Freedom City*, Frederiksted to see where enslaved Africans were bought, sold, then shipped to other Caribbean nations where they picked cotton and cut sugar cane. • You can take a day trip or a romantic sunset sail over to Buck Island to explore the snorkel trail of underwater gardens of coral and see some of the most beautiful tropical fish in the world. • You can fall in love again, or for the first time, while staying at one of our beautiful hotels and small inns like those in this newsletter. Visit their websites to see each of these uniquely different accommodation choices. **The Buccaneer** is one of the world's top fifty tropical resorts, **Innparadise** is a joyous splash of Southern hospitality, and **Carringtons Inn St. Croix**—the ultimate bed & breakfast experience— each with spectacular views!

St. Croix is the Caribbean island where history, culture and the performing arts come together to create a once in a lifetime magical experience.

Celebrities at InnParadise

Actor Danny Glover in center

Actor Glynn Turman, 3rd from left

Chapter 15
How it Ended

We began thinking about returning to the states earlier than our planned ten years. The grandkids were growing up and we wanted to be a part of their early lives. Business was dwindling for most tourist related businesses.

In the interim of trying to sell the property, we became a vacation rental and my dear "sistah" Naita managed the property. It took almost two years to sell InnParadise. We sold it as a residence, not a business.

We settled back into our lives in Atlanta. Tommie's loyal customer base was still intact and they were waiting for him with their jobs lists ready. The closing date was established; but we had a conflict. Tommie had just signed a contract to do a sizable job and was not available to return to St. Croix with me. My goodness...what am I going to do?

After much discussion, we decided to offer someone an opportunity to have a "working" vacation in the islands. We thought that would be a win-win for someone. All they had to do was get there. They would mainly assist me in a gigantic yard sale and in clearing out the property.

Our dear friends Wayne and Julia jumped at the chance to go with me. Wayne is an avid golfer and welcomed the chance to play the course at the Buccaneer Hotel. It is a par 70, 18-hole golf course encompassing 5,668 yards with spectacular views of the Caribbean Sea from 13 holes. My agreement with him was that he would be connected with our golfer friends. Julia loves the beaches and so do I; so, that worked nicely.

We worked hard and played hard as well. It worked out great and I was glad to get to share some of our island experiences with them since they did not get to stay with us when we were officially in business. Mission accomplished!

Overall, it ended up being not as financially profitable as we had hoped. However, the experience was invaluable.

It was bitter sweet to return to the states because we dearly loved the people we met, the rich culture and history of St. Croix. We had also discovered our mission/ministry …. that of hospitality. So before leaving it was clear that this was our training ground and only the beginning.

Upon returning to the Atlanta area, our sister, Kitty, gave us a jar with the caption "HOPES & DREAMS." She said that this was to inspire us to move forward with the next venture. We have placed within that vessel our DREAMS, HOPES AND THE POSSIBILITIES for our future.

And here we are today, August 9, 2013. A dear friend of mine, Tony, had recommended that I read "The Dream Giver" by Bruce Wilkinson[3]. It was on my bookshelf; but only partially read. I took Tony's advice and devoured it this time! This book had been a gift to me and what a gift it has turned out to be!

---

[3] Wilkinson, Bruce. The Dream Giver. Colorado: Multinomah Group, 2003.

After reading it, I realized how important it is for me to continue to embrace my dreams. I am ready to move out of my Comfort Zone being aware of the Bullies I might encounter along the way. As I move in faith, I am so excited about what lies ahead knowing that it is all good and it is all God!

ABOUT THE AUTHOR

Paula Smith Broadnax

Paula is actively involved in the Cancer Support Ministry at Greenforest Community Baptist Church in Decatur, GA. She is a former member of "Shades of Pink," an Atlanta based choir comprised solely of breast cancer survivors. Paula is also a member of Sisters by Choice which is a cancer support group founded by her breast surgeon, Dr. Rogsbert Phillips-Reed.

Paula contributed to a book entitled *"Sisters on The Journey"* which was edited by Rev. Dr. Regina Anderson and published by Sisters on the Journey, Inc. This book consists of short stories written by women who have opened their private lives to the world revealing God's assurance of His agape love. Her piece is entitled "This Little Light of Mine."

After spending five years on St. Croix living her dream, Paula and Tommie, her husband of 17 years, returned to Georgia to be an active part of the lives of their thirteen grandchildren.

Paula Smith Broadnax resides in Ellenwood, Georgia, an Atlanta suburb.

You may find her on Facebook and
http://paulasmithbroadnax.com
http://dreamshopesandpossibilities.com

Paula Smith Broadnax